YOUR KNOWLEDGE HAS VALUE

- We will publish your bachelor's and master's thesis, essays and papers

- Your own eBook and book - sold worldwide in all relevant shops

- Earn money with each sale

Upload your text at www.GRIN.com
and publish for free

Bibliographic information published by the German National Library:

The German National Library lists this publication in the National Bibliography; detailed bibliographic data are available on the Internet at http://dnb.dnb.de .

This book is copyright material and must not be copied, reproduced, transferred, distributed, leased, licensed or publicly performed or used in any way except as specifically permitted in writing by the publishers, as allowed under the terms and conditions under which it was purchased or as strictly permitted by applicable copyright law. Any unauthorized distribution or use of this text may be a direct infringement of the author s and publisher s rights and those responsible may be liable in law accordingly.

Imprint:

Copyright © 2017 GRIN Verlag, Open Publishing GmbH
Print and binding: Books on Demand GmbH, Norderstedt Germany
ISBN: 9783668613065

This book at GRIN:

https://www.grin.com/document/387416

Silvia Stamenova

The latest EU-Commission President Elections and the role of the European Parliament

GRIN Publishing

GRIN - Your knowledge has value

Since its foundation in 1998, GRIN has specialized in publishing academic texts by students, college teachers and other academics as e-book and printed book. The website www.grin.com is an ideal platform for presenting term papers, final papers, scientific essays, dissertations and specialist books.

Visit us on the internet:

http://www.grin.com/

http://www.facebook.com/grincom

http://www.twitter.com/grin_com

The latest EU-Commission President Elections and the European Parliament's role in them

Outline

The question posed in this paper relates to the latest EU-Commission President Elections and the European Parliament's role in them. The examination of this question is imperative since recent literature on the subject has regarded the situation of the democratic deficit within the Union as simply "putting a little more weight" on the average's citizen's vote by convincing them that they are also voting for not just national representatives, but for Commission President, as well. Unfortunately, this is a matter usually ignored in today's studies on the subject. This paper, therefore, describes the whole election process and explains the election process in 2014 (Jean-Claude Juncker), all specifications, all differences and circumstances. However, it gives some interesting conclusions on what the EP's real motivation was? However, it is not clear whether it was power, policy or democracy. If we take for granted that different motivations might have existed, and ask why the European Council accepted the Spitzenkandidaten procedure, we will reach some interesting conclusions. Formally, the Council is in charge of nominating the Commission president, and member states until then have always wanted to keep this privilege. Hence, exploring the issue what important member states said about the EP's initiative, how they reacted, and why some of them in the end gave their assent will be beneficial for the essay.

Research question

In general, the election process in 2014 was part of significant change that was called "Spitzenkandidaten". In its core, this concept basically represented the introduction of rival candidates from the different European-level parties. The idea behind this change was to transform the European elections in such a way that they resemble the ones conducted on national level in the different member states. However, it gives some interesting conclusions on what the EP's real motivation was? However, it is not clear whether it was power, policy or democracy. If we take for granted that different motivations might have existed, and ask why the European Council accepted the Spitzenkandidaten procedure, we will reach some interesting conclusions. Formally, the Council is in charge of nominating the Commission president, and member states until then have always wanted to keep this privilege. Hence, exploring the issue what important member states said about the EP's initiative, how they reacted, and why some of them in the end gave their assent will be beneficial for the essay.

1. Introduction

The European Commission, being a part of the European Union's organs, usually takes on a number of different tasks. So as to fulfill them it has to be headed by the right person and to be governed in accordance with the relevant procedures. Hence, the process of nominating and electing a Commission President is one of the processes requiring greater attention. The post of a Commission President was established in the distant 1958 and each of the candidates has to be nominated by the European Council so that in a later stage he or she can be formally appointed by the European Parliament for a period of five years. However, once elected the president of the Commission is held responsible for the actions of the Commission in front of the Parliament.

In order a political figure to be considered in the nomination process he or she does not necessarily have to be a leading national politician. However, reforming the work of the commission in a time of difficult political choices will call for a strong president (Janning, 2014). The "Spitzenkandidaten" campaign, in which the major parties each nominated their own candidate for commission president ahead of the results of the vote, represents a counter-revolution in terms of institutional politics. The European Commission's president is proposed by the European Council. Until 2004, the traditional approach to choosing the president was through bipartisan agreement on a common candidate between the core countries around the Franco-German centre. But in 2004, the European People's Party (EPP) carried out a coup. In that year, EPP leaders successfully caucused before the European Council meeting to agree on placing their own candidate at the helm of the European Commission, overturning the previous consensus approach (Janning, 2014). Furthermore, what is believed to now play a role in the motivations of the different parties was replaced by the procedure of "Spitzenkandidaten".

2. The election process

As abovementioned the subject of the analysis will be the previous elections, namely those of 2014. Simply put, the latter will be done via the purpose of examing the changes that have taken place in the act of choosing a Commission president. The most significant change that took place in those election was the procedure of "Spitzenkandidaten". Literally meaning "lead candidates", it basically represented the introduction of rival candidates from the different European-level parties. In 2013, the S&D proclaimed Schulz as "Spitzenkandidat", the party's choice for head of the European Commission. The Liberals and Greens followed their example with their nominations by forcing the EPP to nominate their own frontrunner, tying their hands with regard to manoeuvring within the European Council. As a matter of fact, that was the first stage of the so-called by Janning "silent revolution"; and indeed it was silent. What I mean is that all the rhetoric and public attention was focused on the selling proposition of strengthening European democracy by giving voters a choice on who would lead the EU's executive body (Janning, 2014).

It should be noted that the idea standing behind this change was to transform the elections in Europe in such a way that they would resemble the ones conducted on a national level in the various member states. While the people give their vote for a specific party in the parliamentary elections, they can also vote for a person, a figure that in a case of future win could head the newly-formed government. So, the concept of "Spitzenkandidaten", being based on the same principle would thus facilitate and popularize the democracy in Europe.

The first elections, introduced in the European Union, in 1979 raised the hopes that the policy making would gain more in legitimacy if the organs responsible for the legislation were held accountable for their actions by the European citizens and respectively by the voters. In time and through series of legal acts, the European Parliament managed to gain more powers, using the argument for the need of more legitimation of the Union, as it is the organ elected by the people, in exchange for its agreement to cooperate with the policies conducted by the Council.

However, it was interesting to trace what really happened after the introduction of the "Spitzenkandidaten" procedure; the S&D and EPP factions claimed the chances to win a majority of the house to Juncker. The Prime Minister of the United Kingdom David Cameron rejected Juncker on grounds of lack of qualifications and violation of the privileges of the European Council. The core of the Union, the German Chancellor Angela Merkel represented Juncker as one of the good candidates among the several others; eventually, she gave him her support due to the Cameron's intransigence, the steadfastness of the EPP MEPs, and Juncker's determination not to step aside. As a result the entire set of top European posts has become subject to negotiation (Janning, 2014).

On the contrary, the motive behind "Spitzenkandidaten" was loudly announced to be able to provide the European citizen with more democratic rights; so that a person who is not an expert on the fuctioning of the European Union would have access to transparency in politics.

However, clearly not enough was done to support such justifications. Undoubtedly, the "Spitzenkandidaten" procedure was here to stay due to the fact that at the next elections in two years, no political group will stumble into the campaign the way they did in the run-up to 2014. Within the political families, the struggle to win the frontrunner position will become more controversial. So, what the real motives behind the "Spitzenkandidaten" procedure really are? Most probably, one of the reasons is the shift of power and authority between European institutions. Naturally, this is a change brought about by the mere process itself. Whatever it is, it is a matter this paper will attempt to analyse.

However, despite the the Grand Coalition style of politics does not by itself address the frustrations and criticisms that have fuelled the fires of Eurosceptic, anti-European parties and groupings. That the two biggest political families have tied themselves to the Spitzenkandidaten process does not represent a landmark of European democracy as such (Jannings, 2014). Moreover, reforming the work of the commission in a time of difficult political choices will call for a strong president. Juncker may not be able to be one – not because he is incapable of it, but because he will face severe constraints. He will not have an open mandate; member state pressure on him will be strong, not least because the member states will be trying to balance the European Parliament's perceived triumph in the nomination process. For its part, the parliament will take every opportunity to remind Juncker of its own role in his nomination, and will seek to increase the attention that the commission pays to issues and ideas raised by parliament (Janning, 2014). So, once again it appears that we have come across the problem named "democratic deficit"; while on the same time the EU's foreign policy instruments will likely remain in many hands with co-ordination too loose to show real effects.

Before the "Spitzenkandidaten" introduction - the open race for Commission President, a race in which the candidates could present their ideas, announce their agendas and make known to the public what type of policies they would follow does not existed. Due to this reason, it was a challenge for the average voter to recognize which party is responsible for a particular policy and which party should be supported. Therefore, the idea of the motivation seen as democracy, would give parliament more responsibilities, namely in the approval of the EU executive figure. Despite the fact, that the Parliament does not have the right to nominate candidates, it made use of the momentum it was given by that change and imposed a decision on leading European parties that they would need to nominate a candidate from their ranks for the position of Commision President. The members of the European Council actually perceived this new tactic as Parliament's attempt to impose its influence on the choice of Commission President, which is actually to be made by the European Council itself.

And hence it came to the elections in question - the ones in 2014. Despite the fact, that they were the first of their kind, the strategy used in them was no new invention, only the motives behind it were obscure. Statistically, the surveys conducted after the 2014 elections showed that there is a room for improvement. However, the voter activity had risen in different countries. Some scholars consider the latter, as more attention was drawn to candidates in particular countries, such as Germany, Luxemburg and France, as they were highly motivated to vote. Others argued that activity had increased in countries which had an economic interest in the prosperity of the Union; namely UK and Greece.

Nevertheless, what is to be accounted for is the fact that these elections were marked by not only a change in treaty, but also by different regional and wide-European outcomes of the 2008 financial crisis. According to a group of studies (Christiansen, 2016) the impact of the Spitzenkandidaten system did not lead to a transformation of the EU's political system. Indeed, rather than creating new opportunities for party political competition, the cooperation between centre-right and centre-left in the election of the Commission President and subsequent decision-making further strengthened the long-standing 'grand coalition' in the European Parliament. Thus, considering these findings it would be reasonable for one to assume that the European citizen views himself or herself as rather a citizen of the member country, and not as one of the Union, so the logical thing to do in the election campaign in 2014 would have been to emphasize the national point of view or angle so that the voter could relate to it. In fact, this is what politicians opted for.

The introduction of the "Spitzenkandidaten" procedure took place against the background of the Eurozone crisis which had polarised opinions about the direction of European integration across the member states. Indeed, there has been gradual change in certain respects, the impact of the Spitzenkandidaten system did not lead to a transformation of the EU's political system.

So far, we have talked about the democracy motive, standing behind the idea of the introduction of "Spitzenkandidaten". However, the supporters of that idea had called for a change in the Lisbon treaty, which would give parliament more responsibilities, namely in the approval of the EU executive figure. Despite the fact, that the Parliament does not have the right to nominate candidates, it made use of the so-called "momentum" and imposed its decision on the European parties. Luckily, that type of proposition was supported by the European Commission, and according to research on public opinion, was welcomed by citizens. On the contrary, the idea was not welcomed by the European Council, who viewed the new tactic as an attempt to impose its influence on the choice of Commission President - task, performed by the European Council itself.

So, simply put, what were the real motivations behind the EP's new procedure? Whether it was power, policy or democracy was a question already discussed in the text above. Despite that, it did not recognizably change the game as one major European institution cleverly used it to tighten its power grasp. Despite the fact that they faced criticism and opposition during the election campaigns, eventually the opponents of the European Parliament came to terms with the EPP's win and supported for at least gave up on the denunciation of the EPP's candidate - Jean-Claude Juncker. The EU's institutional politics remain in a state of flux at a time of continuing internal challenges and new external ones. Both sets of challenges may help to limit the degree of confusion. After all, European integration has mostly taken place only under the pressures of circumstance; it has rarely been ahead of the curve, but it has mostly managed to stay on track. One pattern has not been broken by the revolution: the temptation of European politics to oversell its latest outcome. In this spirit, the Spitzenkandidaten revolution will go into the history books as a leap forward towards a more democratic and accountable Europe (Jannings, 2014).

3. Conclusion

The conclusions being made on the 2014 European elections are several and they are going to be presented in this way; first, the most significant change that took place in those election was the procedure of "Spitzenkandidaten". Noteworthy, is the fact that the idea standing behind this change was to transform the elections in Europe in such a way that they would resemble the ones conducted on a national level in the various member states. While the people give their vote for a specific party in the parliamentary elections, they can also vote for a person, a figure that in a case of future win could head the newly-formed government. So, the concept of "Spitzenkandidaten", being based on the same principle would thus facilitate and popularize the democracy in Europe. Hence, we see the motive of democracy being present.

Second, most probably, one of the reasons is the shift of power and authority between European institutions. Naturally, this is a change brought about by the mere process itself.

Undoubtedly, the "Spitzenkandidaten" procedure was here to stay due to the fact that at the next elections in two years, no political group will stumble into the campaign the way they did in the run-up to 2014. Within the political families, the struggle to win the frontrunner position will become more controversial. Of course, the idea of talks, being accompanied by the necessary noise from the ranks of parliament, by the public positioning and repositioning of governments, and by media analysis and gossiping would perhaps lose its place in the history of modern Europe.

Reference:

Christiansen, T (2016)., "After the Spitzenkandidaten: fundamental change in the EU's political system?", Journal West European Politics, volume 39, 2016, issue 5;

De Vries, C., van der Brug, W., van der Eijk, C. and van Egmond, M. (2011) 'Individual and contextual variation in EU issue voting: the role of political information', Electoral Studies 30(1): 16–28.

European Parliament (2013) 'The power to decide what happens in Europe', available at http://www.europarl.europa.eu/news/en/news-room/content/20130905STO18723/html/The-power-to-decide-what-happens-in-Europe (accessed 20 June 2017).

Føllesdal, A. and Hix, S. (2006) 'Why there is a democratic deficit in the EU: a response to Majone and Moravcsik', Journal of Common Market Studies 44(3): 533–562.

Janning., J (2014) "Five lessons from the "Spitzenkandidaten" European Parliament campaign", European Council of foreign relations, https://web.archive.org/web/20140809192020/http://www.ecfr.eu/content/entry/commentary_five_lessons_from_the_spitzenkandidaten_european_parliament_c281 (assessed 28 August 2017).

Hobolt, S.B and Spoon, J.-J. (2012) 'Motivating the European voter: parties, issues and campaigns in European Parliament elections', European Journal of Political Research 51(6): 701–727.

John Wilson (2014) 'Juncker is the democratic choice to head the EU Commission', Letter to The Guardian, 6 June, available at
https://www.theguardian.com/world/2014/jun/06/eu-democratic-choice-eu-commission
(accessed 20 June 2017).

Michael Shackleton (2017): Transforming representative democracy in the EU? The role of the European Parliament. In: Journal of European Integration Vol.39(2): 191-205, available at http://www.tandfonline.com/doi/abs/10.1080/07036337.2016.1277713 (accessed 20 June 2017).

Open Europe (2014) 'Does Jean-Claude Juncker have a "popular mandate" to become the next President of the European Commission?', Press Release, 12 June, available at http://www.openeurope.org.uk/Article/Page/en/LIVE?id=20223&page=PressReleases (accessed 20 Juni 2017).

Sara B. Hobolt (2014): A vote for the President? The role of Spitzenkandidaten in the 2014 European Parliament elections. In: Journal of European Public Policy Vol.21(10): 1528-1540

Schimmelfennig, F. (2014) 'The Spitzenkandidaten plot: the European Parliament as a strategic competence-maximizer', available at
http://europedebate.ie/spitzenkandidaten-   plot-european-parliament-strategic-competence-maximizer/ (accessed 20 June 2017).

Thomas Rogers (2014) 'Commission crusade: Cameron outmanoeuvred in battle over Juncker', Article to Spiegel Online.19 June 2014. available at http://www.spiegel.de/international/europe/cameron-and-juncker-fight-over-role-in-european-commission-a-975528.html (accessed 20 June 2017).

YOUR KNOWLEDGE HAS VALUE

- We will publish your bachelor's and master's thesis, essays and papers

- Your own eBook and book - sold worldwide in all relevant shops

- Earn money with each sale

Upload your text at www.GRIN.com and publish for free